ON YOUR JOURNEY

Words of Light and Life

ON YOUR JOURNEY

Words of Light and Life

BY MARLON P. WEAVER

Editor:
Aimee Huffstetler

Photos:
Melinda Manzo

aths

$\mathcal{F}$oreword

THERE ARE MANY ways to improve, accomplish goals, even move forward, and "On Your Journey" is intended to be a light while you are looking to take the steps that are just right for your personal path. Whether you look back to learn from something that you have already gone through, or look ahead with a new understanding of what you can do, or even stand still to look all around and know that you are exactly where you need to be, understand that you just made a life decision towards being the "best" you.

The thoughts and words in this book are a collection of wisdom and inspiration that reflects the experiences of life, and can be a timeless resource for navigating your personal circumstances. Each quotation may hold a different meaning every time that it is read. One line may seem simply unique, just for you; wherein that same moment be life changing for another person.

These original quotes are an extension of my previous book, "Onward," and are part of the real conversations, about the *good, bad and best* of times that are shared with the people you meet on the way. This book is yours to open up to any page on any day and discover something new. As you journey from the Title, through the Table of Contents, to the last words written, you will discover new meaning every-time. Revisit your favorites or take notes as you please, enjoy finding insight today that can be used for tomorrow.

This book is not perfect; there are misspelled words, inadvertent errors, over punctuations or none at all. I intentionally chose to leave it this way to represent that every road traveled is not perfect and may need to be traveled again in order to be better.

Let this book be a guide as you walk, run, or fly *On Your Journey*.

$\mathcal{D}$edications

THIS IS A SPECIAL dedication to my daughter Jenna, who makes me proud and inspires me to remain humble, grateful and consistent. Her integrity, spirit and heartfelt desire to be a positive influence is recognized by everyone who knows her. I know that she will continue to do great things and be a light of good for all to see.

This is a special dedication to the people who, throughout tremendous circumstances, were essential workers during a time of crisis. In a uniform or not and in every capacity imaginable, you served our communities and country at every level, even to the point of being placed in harms way to keep us safe. Your compassion, commitment and sacrifice is greatly appreciated and will never be forgotten.

This is a special dedication to parents, educators, and leaders; you help us to grow, navigate and work in the world around us. Thank you for setting the example and showing us that words and actions should compliment one another. You continue to teach us the right way and remain a beacon for us when the way is not so clear.

The Time is Yours

Moments that last a lifetime are good,
but isn't a lifetime of moments
so much better?

Plan the day,
pick a time,
cherish the moment.

Yesterday is a memory, tomorrow is a plan, today is the real opportunity to do the best that we can.

The best thing about today is that we learned from the worst of yesterday to give the hope of a greater tomorrow.

We are told not to dwell in the past, but sometimes being in the present is not working out. If there are good memories in the past, go there and let them help you get through the day.

The essence of time isn't just about what passes by or moves on, the essence of time is about what we hold on to as a memory, shared experience or moment that makes us smile forever.

We keep using up our best years by chasing after what is not best in our life. We can and should have the best years of our life by accepting and appreciating the good that comes to us day by day.

Take a chance. This time go for yours and don't let the first of what you want be the last of what you choose.

Good Lighting

I'm enjoying my four-leaf clover
one leaf at a time.

My goal for the day is to commit a bunch of random acts of smiling.

Have a song for a day.

Welcome your Friday with open arms.

Every day there is one more thing
to be thankful for.

Clip dem antennas, stop the remote
to pieces and get outta control...
laugh a little.

Every breath you take can bring you
one step closer to the best thing
that can ever happen.

Things in life can try to bring me down,
but only so far, because I know what it
feels like to see birds flying beneath me.

Cherish life, enjoy the treasure of love appreciate every happiness and make time to have fun. Every day is your history in the making.

Something good is happening
and it's your turn to have it.

Do you!

If you like to smile and somebody has a problem with it, they always have the option not to look.

Don't let anyone interrupt your joy today. You deserve to be happy and nobody has the right to take that away from you.

Whether we are laughing or crying we are still breathing. In the best times and the worst times, we are alive, and we have the opportunity to make those breaths count.

Shakespeare said, "The world is a stage.", but in our real lives, our happiness does not have to be an act or scripted. Our happiness isn't determined by the applause of others.

Being on either side of laughing
is a gift. Cherish it and most of all,
never stop sharing it because in that
moment of laughing nothing hurts,
worries, or harms you.

Rushing to settle for what you think is happiness is not the way. Do not be afraid; you are not running out of time. Be patient and stand still, give true happiness the chance to find you right where you are.

Your dreams are the chance to be amazing and your life is the chance to make those dreams come true.

Sometimes we need to just lighten up. If we can't laugh at ourselves, give it time; something will happen to make others do it for us.

"H"app"i"ness, think about all of the great things that are the result of saying 'Hi'.

The measure of our happiness isn't always getting what we were looking for, it is also in having our eyes opened to see that we got more, better, even the best of what we deserve. Nothing compares to the happiness of having each other.

Faith for Thought

God moves in our life whether
we believe in him or not...

There is greatness in all of us.
If we replace our greatness with
God's goodness, what exists inside
of us will have a greater effect on
everything around us.

Thank you, Lord for helping when I ask and when I'm not even aware that I need it.

Thank you, Lord for the hard road that
I could not walk on, it helped me
to allow you to carry me over.

Vision gives us the ability to see around, ahead, and inward. Looking around is how we project, looking ahead is how we predict, and looking inward is how we perceive. When Jesus healed the blind, He made them better, He opened their eyes to see what's around them, but also gave them the ability to see what is inside of them. Today, see yourself as better because what is around you won't matter as much when you can look inside of yourself and what is ahead of you is greatness.

Maybe I look into things too deeply,
but some things are too amazing to
be 'just coincidence'. The purpose is
for God to know, the experience
is for us to enjoy.

Faith and trust seem similar but they're truly different. Trust is reactive, the byproduct of time and experience. Faith is proactive, the expectation of a just-in-time experience. Let these two work in conjunction. Have faith in God and learn to trust Him.

Let's be encouraged to continue to pray for the families and for each other and unite against the spirit of fear that causes us to look at each other like enemies. There are very serious and real problems in this world, and in this country and the only way to effectively deal with it is by effectively dealing with ourselves. This is a human problem and it only takes making one change and one choice at a time to make a difference. We need strength and courage to make those types of choices and to avoid giving in to whatever influences us to continue to be part of the problem. Let's take the first step to being part of the solution by doing this... think about at least one person that you love and think about what it would take to make their lives better, one choice at a time.

Being strong isn't about pointing out the weaknesses of another, it is about recognizing that we are all weak. Only by God helping us, and us helping each other can we be strong.

It has been said that it only takes one
bad apple to spoil the bunch, but
it only took one good apple to give
every other apple a second chance.
Thank you, Jesus.

Do not underestimate the strength of a woman; remember, man was made from dust and woman was made from bone.

At this stage I am learning that it's not about the big moves or great gains, it is more about the little things like sharing the breaths, memories and precious moments of time with people you love. It is about being afraid to take a step but having the faith that God won't let you fall. It is reaching out to continually hold hands. Start by saying hello, finish by never letting go.

Life is Beautiful

Beauty does not fade with age; it becomes seen more clearly by those who understand and appreciate it.

On the face, some years and a little gray for the hair shows I did that and been there. Good memories behind me, life all around me, and living ahead of me.

Is it true that some of us don't act the age that we look, but it is way better than looking the age that we feel.

My youth isn't gone, even though my wrinkles tell something different. My heart stays fresh and available for something consistent.

Beauty exists whether or not it
is heard, seen or felt. There are
many who experience it without
recognizing it. Listen for it, look for it
and reach for it. You will be amazed
to discover it was sitting next
to you the whole time.

Stop Look and Laugh

Tryna get it crackin' like
some ashy elbows.

I look like a bum today and I'm
fine with that. I give everybody else
permission to look good for a change.

Someday this will be on a t-shirt: "Notice: I've filled the position as my own worst enemy; your service is no longer required!"

Open up and Answer

What is a positive change that
you have made in your life?

What would you like to accomplish
before the month is over?

What was your first job?

I would like to...

Sometimes I just miss...

Make a wish.

Is there one thing in this world
that you want more of than
you already have?

What are your back in the day
Saturday memories?

You thought you had a match made in heaven, but soon found out it was a first date from hell. Share your creative ways to end the date early:

I would have gone into work today but...

You have done everything right
and the interview is almost over,
however, the burritos that you had
for dinner last night just came back
with a vengeance. How do you
distract yourself to avoid potential
catastrophe?

Do you have a nice personality?

Your purpose, your destiny, your happiness is trying to find you but can't recognize you. Do you feel like you have to be somebody different just to be yourself around everyone else?

Are you not seeing something about you that is amazing because you are still trying to find the non-existent flaw that somebody else said was there?

What is the purpose of ever telling
your story to people who can
never relate?

Is settling in a relationship self-inflicted abuse or the reflective observation of a decision gone wrong?

Would you rather cry silently in a mansion or laugh hysterically in a shack?

Friendship

Instead of being the voice of reason,
try being the ear of understanding.

We may not always understand how someone feels, but we can listen so they know we are trying.

Someone you know would be blessed to receive this message: "Hey, would love to catch up sometime. Let me know if you want to grab some lunch."

Kindness usually travels forward and gets lost on the way back. Some people are the well-placed landmarks that help kindness find its way back.

Just because you stand out
doesn't mean you stand alone.

Some people come around to be encouraged and some come around to be an encouragement.

Somebody is going through what you just came out of. Be a light and show them how to make it.

How good a person is will not be determined by how well liked they are or how much thanks or appreciation they receive. How good a person is will be based upon their willingness to do the right thing for the sole purpose of doing the right thing.

It is good to spend a lifetime making friends, even better to spend a day being a friend.

Anybody who couldn't hang around during the process really does not deserve to enjoy the benefits of the end results.

Why are we fighting about what's worth losing when we should be losing what's not worth fighting about?

It is true that the way we communicate now is different, however, when the electronics fail, we will have to rely on face-to-face human interaction. Don't ever lose the ability to be upfront, smile, shake someone's hand, and look someone in the eye when we talk.

The world is full of people who are selfless, honest, good, and loving. If you have trouble finding someone like this, be their blessing.

Here is a shout out to the people in your life who don't judge you but will always call you on your BS. They won't lend you money, but they will share their groceries, and goodness forbid, if you ever robbed a bank, they will tell you how stupid you are as they drive the getaway car. These are your true friends. They have problems of their own, but they always make room for you and yours.

We all have shortcomings. When noticing someone having a setback, instead of making things worse, let us use what we've learned from our trials to help them overcome theirs.

Whether you pray, visit, chat, text or go to lunch, continue to look out for one another. This is what we do, this is what makes us better human beings.

Hunger doesn't take a break,
neither should breaking bread.

It is better to say what needs to be heard than to have heard enough of what was said.

The kind of words that inspire you to think, believe and smile are timeless. More importantly, the kind of actions that make those words true are without a doubt priceless.

Do not offer advice, security, I told you so or even opinions. Just your presence when they need it the most and at least the understanding that you are there when they don't.

Let us see 1+1 as more than 2. Let us see it as 11, observing two number ones walking side by side.

Allowing people in your life who do not recognize your worth and who make you feel like you have to prove yourself is not the answer. People who come into your life that appreciate who you are provide worth that doesn't need to be questioned.

Love is the Way

Love should not be treated like currency; it is way too valuable to use just to get what you want.

Share a kiss at one second til
midnight so that you can end
one day and start another with
the person you love.

Life is short and sometimes so is love, but the distance between the two does not have to be. Here is your moment, do what you need to do.

Saying 'hello' to family while you're saying goodbye to a family member is difficult but being thankful for every member of your family is easy.

Laughing and crying are separate
expressions of the heart, but when
experienced at the same time,
demonstrate the impression
on the heart.

Good parenting involves showing your children how great they are to you.

Waiting for the right time is only half
as important as making
the time right.

The need to be liked and loved
is natural, however, do not allow
someone to feed of your ability to
give those things until there is none
left. They will never return that love
because they can't, it was never in
them to start. You deserve better.

Take a look in the mirror. The person you see there has been waiting a long time for the chance to get to know you better. Let them; that person is the love of your life.

The point when you realize that so much of you has been wasted on someone who does not care about themselves is when you come to understand that part of you needed to be dropped so that the real you can shine.

Truth, love and pain can all hurt. One of these makes you too weak to care; that's not how it is supposed to be.

Beauty is not in the eye of the beholder, value is. Beauty is in the spirit of the object, which is priceless.

Just because the heart is meant to keep beating, doesn't mean it deserves to take one.

Consider this about who you love:
10 years with you is not enough and
10 minutes without you
is way too much.

A relationship takes work, but that
doesn't mean it has to be a job.

Sometimes you have to avoid saying hello to someone because goodbye is soon to follow.

A work of art and your smile are similar. Seeing every detail makes it possible and what makes it priceless.

Love is more of a puzzle than it is
a picture. It is much better to put
pieces together to make something
beautiful than it is to take something
beautiful and break it to pieces.

No matter what you do to put the wrong puzzle piece in place, even reshaping it, when you step back to look at the picture you will see that it doesn't belong there. If you step back and see that someone doesn't belong, allow them to leave. Your picture is too good to include something that doesn't fit.

Know your worth! Sacrificing for love is much better than sacrificing because of it.

Relationships should not be
accessories awards, or trophies.
Relationships should be
the case that displays your
accomplishments together.

The human heart beats over 100,000 times per day, it only takes one beat to show someone that you love them.

Don't throw away or overlook "good" just because you didn't think it was "good enough" because you end up missing out on "great" which was in progress the whole time.

Some people wear their heart on their sleeve, they care and give unselfishly. Stop taking advantage of these people. If you can't reciprocate or pay them back, and least show appreciation and say thank you.

Break-ups, death, divorce, loss of
employment, and injuries can be
hard to overcome physically and
emotionally. These things can happen
suddenly and leave long lasting scars,
but this does not have to be the
end of our story. There is something
inside of us that makes us unique.
Use that as the starting point to reset
yourself and become strong again.
Make the promise to yourself that you
will not be lost to setbacks but will
reintroduce yourself to the world
in your get back.

Love costs everything, but as poor
as you become for obtaining it, the
richer you are for having it.

"abcd E fgh I jk L mn O pqrst U V wxyz" No matter how you look at it, L-O-V-E will always keep U and I together.

There are two parts to love. There is the unselfish part that we share with others, but more importantly, there is the 'selfish' part which is the agreement that we make to ourselves to only allow the people in our lives who make it better.

Rejection is a matter of perspective. You may have been turned down or looked over, saving you from something potentially bad to keep you available for something greater.

You don't have to settle or limit
yourself, but please realize that you
can find at least one exception
with every expectation.

Letting someone else do for you can be hard but doing for yourself when you are not supposed to and messing things up in the process makes things a lot harder.

I am a big person and I have big eyez, which help me to see beyond someone's faults and help with carrying their burdens when necessary.

Instead of holding onto the ghost of our happy, reach out toward the hope of happiness; loving in the future is much better than living in the past.

When all you have to offer is your broken pieces, they can love you one piece at a time. You both can share your broken pieces and put them together to make someone new, someone who is made specifically for each other.

Perhaps you find that things have been broken or shattered just like a mirror. Realize that it may be better to leave that situation alone than hurting yourself trying to pick up those pieces.

Love is big enough to be found
everywhere and still small enough to
fit in the space between
two held hands.

You are the moon to me, I would make my way up, up, up just so that you can be down with me.

Hold hands and take a walk. Each footstep introduces you to a new picture in a slide-show. Look at the sights all around you to enjoy every scene of this wonderful motion picture. When the walk is over, you can look into each other's eyes to see the credits roll. You can watch this movie as many times as you like or plan to see the sequel together.

We feel incomplete because sometimes we try to fill today's void with yesterday's pieces. Let go of yesterday so that there is more room in your hands for what today has for you.

Love can never really be found
because it is never lost. Love isn't
discovered because it isn't hiding.
If it seems like it was lost or hiding,
just look within yourself and you can
appreciate that it has been
with you all along.

Break free from gravity; stop being attracted to distractions and fly to fulfillment.

Each one of us is a living message in a bottle. Think of the heart, how easily it shatters when misused or thrown. Think how transparent it is when there are strong feelings to be communicated. Think about how that bottle, the heart, is safe in the hands of the one who knows how valuable and precious the message inside is.

Was having lunch and one of the place-mats had a word search. A thought came to me: "out of all the letters that could ever be, the only ones that truly matter are UNI."

If you are up front with your crazy,
I may be able to work with that,
but if it occasionally pops out like a
Jack-in-the-Box, don't be surprised if I
carry around a bunch of rocks to keep
on the lid.

The great moments, love in life and happiness in love, are not just fantastic notions but can be a reality if we let them. Somewhere along the line, we learned to anticipate the worse from our best choices. Let's reclaim the good that belongs to us, teach ourselves to expect the best because we deserve it, and enjoy the parts of life that have just been waiting for us to show up.

I was looking at a candle and thought to myself, it doesn't need to have a perfect "match" to get started, just a reliable heat source. For people, a reliably warm heart is a good place to start.

Would you prefer to be with someone else as the person you are, or be yourself with somebody new?

IF you ask for something that is limitless, like unconditional love, but you hold on to it under conditions, you will not get enough for what you need. Because what you have is already limited, when it is time for you to give, you will find that there is nothing left.

Both of my grandmothers used
to ask us, "What comes first, your
wants or your needs?". In hindsight,
I understand that to them, the only
thing that came first was us.

Somewhere along the way we may feel like we got sidetracked but who we were meant to be, what we were meant to do has never changed. The best thing we can do is be honest by accepting who we are right now and be set free knowing that the best people who love you will always see you at your best.

For every jigsaw puzzle there is also a complete picture of the real thing. Instead of us working so hard to put the pieces of a puzzle together and run the risk of pieces missing. Let's stop breaking up, but rather enjoy holding on to the complete picture of what we have in front of us.

Be the first to be what's wonderful about life; face to face, heart to heart. When every breath becomes more priceless just by saying their name, all that went wrong can finally be right. Be the first to show what LOVE is.

Going backwards will only bring me back to you. Moving forward has eventually brought me back to you. We have moved so far apart, but in reality, we have never left each other's side because our thoughts, hearts, love has always stayed the same. Where do we go from here; stand still, hold hands, and move forward, together.

The ideas and perspectives we have about relationships, especially those that were formed out of trauma, do not fit with our plans to be better. The Ego, being right at the expense of everyone else, and waiting for that bad thing we always knew would happen cannot be part of the told we use to rebuild our happiness.

A good thing about looking in the mirror is seeing the reflection of the person who makes you happy, as well as the reflection of the person standing next to you, who does the same thing.

Relationships take effort. The focus should be less about investing in adding to someone, which is a one-sided approach. The work of investing in and appreciating what is already there is mutually beneficial and will add to everything that a relationship is a part of.

Love in life and happiness in love aren't just fantastic notions, but they can be a reality if we let them. Somewhere along the line we learned to anticipate the worst from our best choices. Let's reclaim the good that belongs to us, teach ourselves to expect the best because we deserve it, and enjoy the parts of life that have been waiting for us to show up.

What is it that we are waiting for? The right time, the right moment, the right person? Something or someone better? How about instead of waiting for these, we become them and enjoy the difference.

I enjoy being wrong; I thought you couldn't be any more beautiful than you were at that moment when I first saw you... then I saw you again.

Onward to Self

A park and a blanket; no shoes,
no socks, no stress.

Greatness is waiting for you to take
the first step; look into the mirror.

I'm too conceited to blame everyone else for my problems.

M set, all good, M fine, my outside
goal iz to fully reflect my inside.

Enjoy today, make memories, start or finish some things. Be thankful to have this opportunity.

Sometimes you just have to get in
the car and ride to some songs.

Take a moment to reflect. You've endured some bad things and you've done good towards others. Only you can decide which of these defines you.

The ability to do good for others is in all of us, but we miss the opportunity because some of us lack the confidence to do good for ourselves. Treat yourself good so in the moment when life needs you to act, you can be great.

It's OK to take some time out for treating yourself to do good.

Today is the day you start to
do something about it.

See yourself for who you really are;
stronger than you think.

The most valuable part of you is not what has been lost, drained or taken away; the most valuable part of you is what remains. You're still standing, you still have joy and you know beyond a shadow of a doubt that everything is going to be alright.

The value of someone doing a good deed for you is priceless, don't ruin that experience for someone else just because you don't value yourself.

You are Saturn and some other people are just the rings; without you they wouldn't even be there.

A mirror will only show you what you've been waiting for; a window will show you everything that has been waiting for you.

We put so much energy into avoiding people. Use that same amount of energy into meeting someone new, doing something new, or being somebody new.

Others who try to make you feel guilty for improving yourself deserve about as much attention as you give the inside of your eyelids when you blink.

If you're the type of person who has the mindset that you want to be better, you are already halfway to where you need to be. The other half is doing better.

Keeping it real isn't about being your worst and expecting people to just deal with it. Keeping it real is about trying to do your best no matter what anybody else thinks.

Look in the mirror and if you don't like what you see, break it. All of the pieces on the ground reflect that there is more to you than you thought.

When it comes to people talking
about you or being haters, just
remember that a dog never barks
at a parked car.

Perhaps we should take a different approach to discovering the meaning of life and discover *a life of meaning.*

There is only one you. Being everyone for everybody will leave you looking in the mirror and not recognizing the person looking back.

Sometimes making the right move
means taking the time to stand still.

Find a goal to run to or be lost to
the obstacle you're running from.

People will not like, help, support, be happy for, or respect you. This makes more room for you to do it for yourself.

A part of you is missing. As hard as it may be, don't try to find it or get it back, don't even replace it. Use that space to grow something new, something that makes you better.

Love yourself! Don't let the ignorance of the environment around make you less than who you really are.

Transforming yourself through weight loss, getting fit, education, financial progress, or spiritual growth is great and takes hard work. Remember that the most important step in all of that is to stay committed to the vision that You have of yourself.

Stand in front of the mirror blind-folded and say at least ten things that you like about yourself. Take the blindfold off and be introduced to a better you.

We have to stop catering to our mistakes because our life isn't about what we have done. We must realize that there is more room for what we can do.

Make a plan, work the plan then
make the plan better so it will work.

Do not let pride stop you from
asking for help.

You don't need to see me to know I'm
doing well; my word is good enough.

Every step of progress now is
one less step of pain later.

I can return a bottle and get back more than your two cents; stay out of my change cup.

When it comes to losing weight,
studying, working, and love; anything
you want to accomplish, give it your
best for 5 more minutes.

Don't worry 'bout it. Your haters are just admirers who won't admit it.

Do not underestimate the power
of your self-respect.

The sky is as blue for you as it is for others. Be free to fly without anyone telling you how far or how high.

Whether you travel through life with your eyes open or closed, there will still be something to learn.

If people want to walk out of your life let them! As a matter of fact, tell them to run so you don't have to deal with them longer than you have to.

If there's something you want to do with your life, make it happen. The truth is, something else will always come up, the money can always be spent on another thing, and there will always be people who won't support you. We are all waiting for the "right" time, but every moment of indecision is time that we can't get back. You are in control of your own happy.

Sometimes it has to be all about you, there is nothing wrong with that and don't let anyone tell you that there is.

You don't have to take the blame
for everything; some things are just
not your fault.

Be a flower! No matter how much dirt
and crap you have to go through, you
will still come out looking
and smelling good.

Overlooking what you need because it does not come wrapped in the expectations of what you want may leave you with receiving neither.

Sometimes it is good to go back
and see yourself.

Settling is what dirt does after it hits
the water. Choose to swim instead.

Success starts with trying.

Setting small goals is good practice
towards achieving great things.

Get up early to drive around and
let the world amaze you.

You are a bird and you can either eat bread or you can eat worms, the main thing is that you have to eat. As a bird, people don't care what you eat, they are more influenced by the way you fly. You just ate a bunch of worms, but you still have the opportunity to fly, so fly! Let the world see you in a way that you forget to see yourself.

Some dayz my dreams get the best of
me, but I am looking forward to the
dayz when I can experience
the Best of My Dreams.

Greet the sun every morning and
invite it to become a part of the rest of
your day. Shine no matter what.

I'm not trying to change the world.
I'm trying to change my life in a way
that makes the world take notice.

Be encouraged. Don't give people the satisfaction to revel in your trials. Your triumph will stop them in their tracks.

Don't let your insecurities masquerade as your inner voice. It is understandable that sometimes they are hard to tell apart, but here is how you can tell the difference: your inner voice's purpose is to guide you through life while your insecurities only seek to hide you from life.

You are not a wristwatch, clock, hourglass, or calendar. Your time is precious, and your worth is priceless.

Someone can't climb a mountain without taking the time to adjust to the change in pressure and oxygen level. It can be that way with situations in life as well. Taking the time to adjust and get stronger on the way makes the view from the top much more valuable.

Don't look back, don't look down, don't even look ahead, instead look at yourself right now. You have the power. Be encouraged to make that work for the rest of the day.

You don't get to be who you really are
if you only surround yourself
with people just like you.

Gravity, as a natural force, is meant to help you stay grounded and give you a way to land after you take flight. It is not meant to hold you down or keep you from going forward. Gravity is also the force of attraction. The same way it works to keep the Earth, the moon and stars together in balance, it can work the same with the people we choose to have around in our lives.

Your dreams are the chance to be amazing and your life is the chance to make those dreams come true.

If the questions the answers and the results seem to be the same, that is because we are the same.

People have the prerogative to not hang on with you through the reality of a situation as it stands right now, however, the best of you is yet to come and it's theirs to miss out on. You are worth more.

Wisdom
(Reflect/Respect/Project)

Walls around, not between.

If a seed could talk, it may say how lonely, dark and scary it was just to make it to ground level; yet how it was worth it all to see the sun and bloom.

Make do with what you do.

Be the wish come true.

Saying hello to someone is not hard work, so don't act like you need to get paid overtime to say hello back.

I have participated on both sides of this particular subject and this is the conclusion that I have come to: tell someone the truth and let them make their own mind up; tell someone a lie and cause them to make things up in their own mind.

Start this day on a positive note and
be sure to have it end on a song.

If you know it is something
that you need to do, do it.

Our life is speaking to us all of the time, don't live it with more regrets than gratitude.

You are still here!

Who knows where the flower grows?
In the ground where it is planted or
perhaps in the vessel where it is most
often watered? I submit that the
flower grows in the fertile heart
of one whose eyes appreciate it.

When you are trying to do good and
all you hear is people saying bad
about you, don't worry about it.
Seeing good will always be worth
more than hearing bad.

Do not accept the negative reaping
of what you did not sow.

The only time our words and actions should not match is if our action will be better than our word.

Things are not always going to be this difficult for you, good things are just one decision away.

Can't be all that you can be by doing less than you should.

Be encouraged when others talk behind your back, it means that you are walking ahead of them.

Don't fear the skunk, just
be aware of its odor.

To have a vision one doesn't need to have eyes, just admit to being a fool, which is the first step to being wise.

Being alive is more than surviving.
Surviving is just eating; living is tasting
and asking for more.

The shortest distance towards
achieving greatness is taking
one step in the right direction.

In life, there are no second chances, just more choices to make. Hopefully the next one doesn't lead to the last one's mistake.

When life hands you lemons, throw
'em back; you don't have to make
lemonade when your water
is already good.

There's nothing wrong with being upset, angry, let down, and having feelings of resentment, but everything right with knowing and showing yourself you are better than that.

Although a leader stands out, they are not a light. They are, however, close enough to light to cast a shadow long enough so that all who see it may be guided towards the light and share in the vision that the leader sees.

Parents: we need to support our teachers. While they are giving our children the education them succeed in the world, they should not become victims of the lack of education we give our kids at home.

In adolescence we can learn all things; in youth we can do all things; at middle age we can teach all things. Let us not wait until we are old in age to enjoy all things.

Our strength is not old measured by how much we can bear, but also how much we are willing to let go of.

The word break affects us in different ways. We break up, we break down, our homes experience break-ins, and sometimes we are just dead broke. Understand this and be encourage that the best part of a break is within our reach; our breakthrough.

Trust is like having a glass of water. If the water spills on the floor it doesn't matter how good or clean the sponge that picks it up is, all of the water will not be put back in the glass. Would you drink the water?

We all have a concept of the way we think things should be, or the way that we want things to be. We shouldn't stop reaching for these things; however, we should consider that life wants something better for us and the road we keep ignoring might just be the road that leads us to our destiny.

When you see the sun, don't stop it from shining. When you see the stars, reach for them.

Do not burn bridges over open water
especially if you cannot swim.

Everybody loves to accept the credit,
but nobody wants to accept the blame.

Sometimes the situation just is what it is, but that doesn't change who we are. Any streak of light in the sky is not a shooting star, real stars don't fall to earth they have a place in the universe where they shine whether it is seen or not.

Trust is not a commodity that can easily be bought and sold. Its value is as priceless as a precious jewel because of how rare it is to find.

Be not afraid of failure, but more concerned about winning with the wrong people on your team.

A lot of us feel intimidated by what we like but do not understand. We may like going to nice restaurants but look at the menu and choose only what is familiar to us, even though there are many other options. We like the idea of being better, but we don't understand the other pathways to improvement. Don't let the thought of progress make you a prisoner to the familiar, instead let it free you to explore all options available to improve your life.

A person's perspective is only as wide as their experiences. You can't expect them to understand where you're coming from if they have never been there or are not willing to go there. This does not make them any more right or wrong, just someone to converse with less as time goes on.

To the person who believes that their life is made better by making someone else's life worse: You can have a lot of money and still be poor. You can make yourself up to look good and still be ugly. You can talk as big as you want, which proves how small you really are. The saddest part of all is that you think this is about somebody else.

Sometimes making a difference
includes not changing a thing.

Experiences, good and bad, shape
our life. How we respond to those
experiences define our life, but to truly
live our life is with no regrets.

The bad experiences that we have had in our life have value too, because those are the things that are our Dream Makers; they help us want better so that we can see better and ultimately do better.

There is a quote that says, "Don't judge a person until you walk a mile in their shoes.", but sometimes those shoes don't fit and there is no way for real understanding. Think about it this way, the ground feels the same to people who don't have shoes at all.

It is OK to be cautious, even wise,
however, if you take the time worrying
about what could go wrong you
may miss what can go right.

We all deserve the opportunity to get a point across, however, the conversation doesn't need to escalate to the point of having an argument. We just need to ask ourselves this simple question do we want to be heard or do we want to be right? If we want to be heard than we can start some dialogue, but if we just want to be right, the conversation is already over.

No matter the situation, it is not hopeless. You don't have to let your guard down, but even when you feel like you don't deserve it, there are people who love you.

For vision to work properly, the signal has to reach the brain and be transmitted back. IT may be that the things we want, need or deserve are right in front of us but we can't see clearly because of what is going on in our head. Don't over-analyze yourself into losing sight of your dreams, blessing, the person to be in your life, or even the person in the mirror.

Don't underestimate the value of zero. Zero equals nothing. Nothing can stop you, bring you down or stand in your way to becoming great.

Arrogance and confidence have some similarities including that they both go a long way, but the major difference is what they bring back.

Being quiet and full of thought is
much better than being loud
with no thought at all.

Something that you say or do today
is going to change somebody's life.

We are told that we can do whatever it is that we want to do and be whatever we want to be. We should continue to be encouraged about those possibilities. It will all be meaningless, however, if the words "good towards others" does not find their way into those two opportunities.

It is a big responsibility to handle trust, but you can do it if you understand how it works. Trust is durable and it is flexible, it can be carried for long or short distance, but once it is shattered, it is extremely difficult to find and put all of its pieces back together.

You don't have to be moving forward to be headed in the right direction. Take a side-step or even back up for your own protection; it can still be all good.

What we *need* knows us better than
what we *want* ever will.

You can do more than what you think;
do more than what you know you should.

Take something good from today
but give something good as well.

Stars are more visible during the night, but they were made to shine all the time.

Anyone that knows me knows that I'm tough, but to be honest, the pain of this recovery seems at times worse than the pain of the injury. When I went in for surgery the doctor made me a promise that I'm going to make a full recovery so every step through this pain of recovery is going to bring me closer to that promise. When you have been promised something in your life and right now all you notice is the pain that you're going through, remember losing things and being injured hurts, but so does the process of healing and recovery. The promises that were made to you are right there waiting for you. All it takes is for you to step through the pain, and eventually step away from the pain so you can step ever closer to your promise.

Step up, step into, step through,
step down if you must,
but never step on.

Let's handle all of our "other" things
that weigh us down and enjoy
the moments that lift us up.

There are two sides to every story, the beginning and the end. Everything in between has yet to be written.

Breaking free of your past may not be as hard as you think. Imagine that you're in a jail cell with no bars, no guards and no locks. The only thing holding you there is that you are standing still and all you need to do to get free is just walk away.

One of the best ways to bounce back after falling flat is to get some fresh air.

It's a shame that some people will shake your hand, but their intent is to steal your fingers.

Don't mistake my kindness for
weakness. It takes a stronger person
to put out a fire than to start one.

Three things are certain:

— Folks will never pay you back!

— You are more available to others than they are for you!

— Nice people don't finish last, they finish best.

Blink more so you don't have
to see them as much.

Don't cry over not being perfect.
Smile bcz you are unique.

Bother because you're not just waiting for it, it is waiting for you. Bother because nothing else has worked so that you can easily recognize and appreciate what does work. Bother because you are worth it all without having to change your worth at all. Bother because you deserve the opportunity to know how it feels to be someone's everything. Bother because taking the chance with the "unfamiliar better" far exceeds staying with the "familiar worse".

Dreams are made at rest, fulfilled
by working, and enjoyed by all
who made them come true.

Amazing isn't just an adventure, it is
your journey, and you will definitely
end up much better than you were
when you started.

MOM. WOW. Whether you are
standing tall on your feet and the
whole world is upside down, or you
feel like you are standing on your
head, when the rest of the world is on
their feet, who you are is absolutely
incredible and what you do is
immensely immeasurable.

Flying would not be interesting if there was only one type of bird. Grow your feathers, soar, and make it happens.

Viewing your progress through the
eyes of your problems will only make
the journey seem insurmountable.
If you, instead, view your problems
through the eyes of your progress,
you will realize that you
have already overcome.

All of us are not called to be diamonds, some are commissioned to remain coal. Although a diamond is tough and can sparkle like the stars, coal is down to earth and when ignited, it provides heat against the coal as well as fire to shine light through the dark.

When you run out of things to say,
draw a picture and that will give
you a credit of a thousand more
words. Putting the pieces of a puzzle
together but somehow there seems
to always be some pieces missing.
Perhaps it may be time to get
a new picture and enjoy
something complete.

Being quiet does not mean giving up, just as being loud does not necessarily mean confidence. The strength of real peace is a result of agreeing to listen and apply what works.

Change isn't instantaneous, it's a process. Change is evident when the world around you looks the same but the way you see the word, more especially, the way you see yourself is different, for the better.

Having all the answers isn't all that matters, neither is asking all of the right questions. What is most important is that we learn to listen whenever either is offered.

You try to smile through every obstacle, just understand that you don't have to, just face them with whatever face you have and before you know it the obstacles will be behind you and your smile will be waiting in front of you.

Don't be so front-loaded that if you fell on your back you could not be pulled up. Don't be so heavy in the back that if you fall on your face you couldn't be lifted up. Be solid so that no matter where the pressure comes from, you will not be moved.

A broad brush can put paint on a
canvas but that will never
be considered art.

The assumption of failing before even trying is already failure. We don't expect a plant not to grow when we put a seed in the ground. The only way that happens is if you don't provide water and light. When we nurture the good things about our life, and in our life, let's also nurture the expectation that good things will grow. The reason why; trying for the good that belongs to you will always outweigh the expectation of failure that does not.

A shooting star isn't a star that falls to Earth, it is light that leaves a trail.

Our life is speaking to us
all of the time, showing us
the best times that are possible;
continue that conversation

Our every decision, good or bad has value. Regrets of those decisions are just the minor cost of embracing the priceless opportunity to change what we need to do.

Ignorance does not have the capacity to accept more knowledge or truth, so don't put effort in trying to explain things. Doing that would be like trying to put food in a bowl with a lid on it. Don't use your energy to take the lid off of what is already rotten. If the ignorant want something intellectual to eat, they need to take off the lid and clean out the bowl themselves. Now let's sit down and have a family meal of intelligence and respect.

Appreciation, consideration, and gratitude shouldn't be used like currency, giving only with the expectation of getting something in return.

Before asking for more out of a situation, we must consider what is missing, lost, or unaccounted for. If the situation turned out to be a 7, for the good or the bead, over something that was a 4, we should accept our part as being the 3.

There are positive aspects of chasing after things, however, if you are chasing after something that means that it could be running away from you. What is truly for you will come to you or meet you while you are on your way.

Every knock on the door is not opportunity. If there is a knock and you go to the door to discover a package has been left behind, that package is considered a message. If you are unable to get to the door, that message could be taken and misused by someone else. Opportunity, however, will knock on the door, the windows, the walls and will even send a draft through the cracks to get you up to come see about it. With true opportunity you may go to the window and see nothing but by the time you get to the door everything that is for you will be made available. Open the door.

The taste of honey in life comes with acknowledging and sometimes accepting the vinegar.

As we bear witness to pivotal moments in history, understand that we all have a part in contributing to, what can become the greatest story of our generation. May our part help to build a stronger foundation, for the home, for the world, that we present to our children...(mweav)

About the Author

MARLON WEAVER, a retired military veteran, credits his parents, family members, and many friends, along with his experiences in the military, for the life lessons, inspiration and positive perspective, which he considers a point of reference and a guide in life. He has published articles in local newspapers, appeared in television news broadcasts, as well as supported the local community through volunteerism, fundraising and charitable donations. He recognizes the teachers of the Waterbury school system and Penobscot Job Corps in Maine as an instrumental encouragement toward reaching his educational goals. Marlon Weaver is a graduate of Eastern Maine Community College, New England School of Communications and Husson University, where he has earned two Graduate Degrees, an MBA and Masters of Education. Originally from Waterbury, Connecticut, he lives in Bangor, Maine along with his daughter and many good friends.

Made in the USA
Middletown, DE
09 April 2023

28310149R00198